Deceiving Wild Creatures

JEREMY OVER was born in Leeds in 1961. He studied law at Leeds University and now lives near Cockermouth in Cumbria, where he works as a policy adviser for the Department for Work and Pensions. His poetry was included in *New Poetries II* (Carcanet, 1999) and his first collection was *A Little Bit of Bread and No Cheese* (Carcanet, 2001).

Also by Jeremy Over from Carcanet Press

A Little Bit of Bread and No Cheese

JEREMY OVER

Deceiving Wild Creatures

CARCANET

First published in Great Britain in 2009 by
Carcanet Press Limited
Alliance House
Cross Street
Manchester M2 7AQ

A CIP catalogue record for this book is available from the British Library
ISBN 978 1 84777 004 2

The publisher acknowledges financial assistance from Arts Council England

Typeset by XL Publishing Services, Tiverton
Printed and bound in England by SRP Ltd, Exeter

For Sophie and Finn

Acknowledgements

Grateful acknowledgements are made to the editors of the following publications in which some of the poems or versions of them first appeared: *Hard Times, PN Review, Poetry Review, Shadow Train, The North, Thumbscrew, The Paper, The Shed* and *Freedom rules: New forms for the making of poems*, edited by David Hart (Flarestack, 2004).

'Whip Tim Kelly' won first prize in the 2002 BBC Wildlife Poetry Competition.

Contents

Epithalamium	9
...and they lived happily until they died.	11
Moustachioed	12
Museum for Myself	14
A Theory of Grasp	16
A New Kind of Kiss	17
Love is not a talent	18
Badly Charred	19
Delight in order	20
Killer in the Rain	22
A Common Pitfall	24
Poetry should be made by all (i)	25
The Lambent Itch of Innuendo	26
Whip Tim Kelly	27
Last Gasp, At the	29
The Waterfall Illusion	30
The Negatives	32
Tree/Bush	33
Blue	34
American Experimental Music	35

Tring	39
The enlargement of the boundaries	40
Not but now and then	41
The exhibition of the fishes	42
Mingles with the forest	43
I only know that	44
Cursu undoso	45
My female moose corresponds	46
of roads.	47
Hard references	48

Your Awful Voice   51
Pastoral   52
And some   55
Poem beginning with a suggestion by Bengt Af Klintberg   56
Being big   57
The Call of the Drum and the Slap of Glory   58
Kabir says   60
A Man in the Wings   61
The Yellow Orioles are equals now   62
Birthday Haibun   63
Several Senryu   65
The North Cumbrian Coast   67
Noses and Feet   69
Leaving me   70
Poetry should be made by all (ii)   71
Pendolino   73

Epithalamium

for Jonathan and Hazel

Rise and put on your foliage, and be seen.
Go in as soon as you are ready.
Our life is short, and our days run
Across streets across countries across reason
And even wolves the sheep forget
How far below thine orb sublime
Described in more detail in
         Claret
         Claret
Bath mat – claret
Once lost can ne'er be found again
Arising spontaneously from the
Aga Whistling Kettle Green

Cynthia, O Cynthia, turn thine ear
Phyllis, Tomalin away
You will live half the year in a house by the sea and half the year in
Bali Paprika pillow cases
Catskill Grabber
Blue Tramline
Or branch: each porch, each door ere this
Plain spoon
Spring, sooner than the lark, to fetch in May
It is not snowing yet but it is dark and may snow yet
Some have dispatched their cakes and cream
Before the appointed time

We peer into the future and see you happy and hope
To be unto him/her a loving and faithful
Acrylic Jam Pot Raspberry
Perky little dog barking in a bar

Never such a merry day
The glasses fell and broke
fresh quilted colours through the air

Joy to that happy pair
Whose hopes united banish our despair
Kingsize – white

...and they lived happily until they died.

She knew him at once and fell weeping upon his neck. Two of her tears fell upon his eyes, which immediately grew quite clear so he could see as well as ever. Everything that he had forgotten came back. He brought up the black poodle with the golden chain, and said, 'this is the villain'. But the duck swam quickly forward, seized her head with her bill and dragged her underwater. Then they leapt over chairs and tables and out of the door and the horse sprang up and dragged the lion away behind him and in his rage he stamped his right foot into the ground so deep that it sank up to his waist. Just then he heard a rustling among the brambles and a golden apple fell into his hand and three ravens flew down and perched on his knee and in a short time she opened her eyes, lifted the lid of the coffin and when they got to mid-ocean, she dropped the nut. On that spot a fine tree sprang up on which the bird rested, then it took them both home where they found their child grown tall and beautiful and the blockhead rode up the glass mountain and ordered more spinning wheels. He was not devoured by wild animals. The grandmother ate the cake and drank the wine and the flies on the walls began to crawl again.

Moustachioed

Seventy years later and we are still just a vaguely connected
series of squiggles sitting in the California sun,
eating our brown bag lunches in Monterey one day
and Eureka the next.

But this is definitely someone.
This is someone's dark-haired wife
looking down from her open window
to the public fountains in the square below.
She is waiting for something – perhaps for that moment
when the bloodstained six-inch iron needles are finally lifted
and basketwork becomes music.

Or perhaps something else. In any event Mrs Williams
– for it is indeed she – is falling asleep now and dreaming
her way into an underwater cartoon adventure.
First she mimics the sounds of a passing turtle,
then a whale, a school of silvery fishes,
a jew's harp, various insects, sirens,
footsteps, fireworks, whaps, slaps
and finally an amoeba spreading
discretely under the lens of a microscope.

Notice the detail, complete down
to the Christmas lights on the shrubbery.
Note too how light from the front door window
spills on to the little front step, underscored
by a quick romping passage on the piano
before the rogue elephant of the orchestra
effs and blinds his way through a sweaty tango;
a springboard of sorts into a steaming bowl of soup
and some rather difficult questions.

Why is it that white and yellow
flowers are the first to appear in spring?
And who do you suppose it was
planted those little seeds of envy in the first place?

I asked David that 'good fer'nuthin cheap fur coat'.
'What is all this? Is it really one of those cinematic sea-changes
as described by historians in Chesapeake Bay?
Or is it simply a case of dropping
Martini glasses, one by one, off the edge of the sideboard?'

His hand reached into the bedroom
and rifled through the books with diabolical glee
searching for all the rhythms and symbology, the whole caboodle
and a climactic scurry across the banquet table
towards a mouthwatering tower of cheesecake.

And beyond that, perhaps, some quieter days
where we might go out to the backlot lake
and engage in a spot of illegal carp fishing.

Museum for Myself

for Peter Blake

Getting up, going out and talking to people are all part of it
one thing stuck to another from left to right
à nos victimes civiles et militaires
I will trawl around the toyshop
Typography

with the wrestlers
thoughts are things
as a little boy holding an image of himself as a man
as much as a brush is
bread   poultry   Ave Maria

a display of hats plays a crucial role
a sort of safety valve
Gayton Vicarage, Sonny Liston, hernia belts, student songbooks
                                                    and dog food
acquired 1967

The extraordinary talents and generosity of Peter Blake
bits of wire and allusions to reproduction for Oxfam
a miracle visible in the work of the infinite
kinds of salami, an obituary cushion, the parents' bedroom,
Dumdie Doodles, the dissecting table and the umbrella Tuesday
introduced by fireworks so deftly
that the join is invisible   a tennis ball
painted to represent Ely Cathedral
or Dorothy
or a privet hedge questioning children
about, on the subject of, and approximately Eduardo
Paolozzi shaped like a battleship
every corner a great joy

So far so good
Everything is coming to an ordered conclusion
Knowledge was accumulated with care and difficulty to this end

No, I don't think so. No, not any more. No.
Not really.
It was. It could have been.
But I don't know. It depends.
Maybe in the past few years. Partly.
In a way, yes. Quite a bit. I think so.
Yes, Yes. I do, Yes.
Oh Yes.
Yes both.

A Theory of Grasp

Verily verily
he that cannot be changed
and become as a little child
with a jarring clamp
in the eyeballs
leaves you exhausted

Rain and snow
do drop from the air
mit goose-bumps in the ditch
flattened under our persuasive
but crouching summary

The canal
as noted above
an unpleasant itch
for the moribund fruit of poodles

And so briefly
with some sniffing at the fingers
in the sublime belief that no one is ever looking
it soon became the vogue on 10th street
to say 'terrific' with a Dutch accent

I've never looked back in that respect
Ralph Eugene Meatyard
Beef Tomato on the upper deck (no. 11 Friday mornings)
and the general public is left fresh in boxes of ice
For the Beauty of the Earth
confronted by a writhing sea of Hildas
all collecting glass in hampers
and carrying them into church
to provide additional illumination.

A New Kind of Kiss

This was how it seemed
He stood still
Whispering footmen
Peppermint drops
A soft lilac laugh
A moustache
A crack in the mazurka
and on his left a new shame.

He was on the point of poplars
as, with the first door, he realised
he had convinced himself backwards.

He was lost, he was beyond, he was darkly lit,
and his hands worked the billiard room.
'I love this so much,' he said, adjusting his neck.

Love is not a talent

I said 'Let's undress' and she put her head sideways
and said 'Um' quietly in the kind of light I would sometimes see
when swimming underwater in a blue Botticelli robe
under a hemisphere of cloud scenery filled with an ever-moving
train of changing, melting forms of every colour
all vanishing away...

There must be no vagueness.
I want Patricia and I want a dog
and so I do a dog and then

I do another dog and so
I *am* the other dog.

I am very fond of the girls taking it easy
just below the prophets.

Thoughts on RISING MOON with raving-mad splendour of orange
                                                  twilight glow:
my fingers emit sparks of fire with expectation of my future labours.
They are fireflies – the little bits of me thrown freely about...

My behaviour is quite difficult.
Fish dart in and out of the coral reef.
A green parrot is also a green salad and a green parrot.

As I walked in the snow I felt as if she was talking through the wall.
No one was in any hurry.
Here and there things slowly moved off.

A continuous parcel-opening experience leaks
through loopholes in the thickest shade.

The letters dot the grass like wildflowers.
I so to speak ensnare them.

Badly Charred

Two burglars are cycling along on a wet and windy night and brimming over with useful information beyond the highlands of Kashmir immortalised by obesity during the long winter evenings. They call at the house of a friend. Walk sideways. Tied hand and foot. Fall. So too the people. It is often a balancing act.

I would like to dance with a heavy curtain. I would like to sail with a shipload of wire fasteners. I would like to be enraptured with stray glimpses of the snowclad ridges that could only be reached in time by drawing out a coil of rope with a fairly feeble Northumbrian girl, the ill-fated Indian chief and a terrific chat about lizards.

The famous teeth of his lordship complied with all of our wishes some feet below the rapid birdlike swooping of the men on skates. Months pass, years even. People from different countries are not really very efficient and on examining the spoor were only talking of Salzburg. Over the garden wall the invisible man is washing his car full of game. He has never seen such a miserable bunch of animals.

Outside the twelve-mile radius she was still on her knees among the alders stocking what seemed like just so many paper bags. It is a place where fat and table merge. So I walked on. A kernel of truth distracted by the raven's cry. She said she was damned small. A crack appeared in the ceiling. A one-time baroque interior breaks down in mountains of salt. Swamp salesmanship. Lamp posts. Milk. A glass of milk is supple.

Alone in my hut I put on pyjamas and climbed into bed. I began to brood and looked at the badly charred chair. Transient disturbances of consciousness run the risk of confusion with petit mal. To make art which doesn't sit on its ass in museums but which prompts a rediscovery of the world, like Eartha Kitt's Englishman, takes time. This is merely the tip of the iceberg.

Delight in   order

Erased Herrick

i
  sweet
Kindles in

        crimson
     neglect
      do   confuse

  the
     shoes

          .

ii
A wee
           wanton

       tract

    all   stomach
  cuff   and
      flow

Do more bewitch me than hen art
        .

iii
A
            clot   on
A lawn

                              here and there

A   ning   a   ving

A careless   hose

Do   itch me   art
    too   part.

iv
                              dress
        in

        fine
            lace
                    son
                    and

            wave

                    string

    more   than
                    ever   .

21

Killer in the Rain

after Raymond Chandler

I

'Who did you say you was?' I snarled.
He thought it over,
'Skip it,' he snapped.
This was an hour or so later.

He thought it over,
then we went back to the living room.
This was an hour or so later.
Then we all went back to the bar.

Then we went back to the living room.
'Get them fleas outa your pants,' she growled.
Then we all went back to the bar.
'What you doin here?' he asked gruffly.

'Get them fleas outa your pants,' she growled.
That didn't get her anywhere.
'What you doin here?' he asked gruffly.
'Money in the bank,' she croaked.

That didn't get her anywhere.
'Skip it,' he snapped.
'Money in the bank,' she croaked.
'Who did you say you was?' I snarled.

II

Nothing more happened.
I had another hunch.
I poked it under her nose,
then I ran away.

I had another hunch
that stopped the door closing,
then I ran away.
I don't know why

that stopped the door closing.
'Nuts,' I said leaning forward.
I don't know why.
I could see a metal bracket that supported the porch.

'Nuts,' I said leaning forward
but it didn't work.
I could see a metal bracket that supported the porch.
'We're going at this wrong,' she said.

But it didn't work.
I poked it under her nose.
'We're going at this wrong,' she said.
Nothing more happened.

A Common Pitfall

is floating on a clear pond
with a gleam in its eye
characterised by excessive reaching
grabbing and lunging for
the Seven Habits of Highly Effective People
1. Flex the elbow and wrist slightly
2. Use a mat
3. Keep it positive
etc, etc.

It really is easier than you thought isn't it –

guage
gulation
gling flow

a flamingo taking flight
or Meryl Streep
is something
you either have
or you don't
as the balls go flying
in all directions.

Poetry should be made by all (i)

1. Always warm up beforehand, stretch your head forward, backwards, sideways – anything to warm up the muscles in your neck.
2. Then, stand before a mirror and repeat the alphabet. The lips should be about a quarter of an inch apart and the jaws held firmly fixed. For B the letter G should be substituted. For P use the letter K. The letter V can be treated similarly to F by breathing hard.
3. When you're ready close your eyes and take a deep breath.
4. Lift your knees waist high. Touch the floor outside your left foot, between feet, circle bend backwards as far as possible and slap your chest at the same time as twisting to touch your right elbow to your left knee and vice versa before dropping to a half-crouch position with both feet, thighs and chest completely off the floor.
5. Maintain this position for the count of ten ensuring the legs and arms are kept straight.
6. Sit up just far enough to see your heels and imitate the playing of a banjo by saying 'Ping', 'Pang', and 'Pong', for the notes and sending the sound through the nose.
7. Now try the tearing of calico by sharply drawing the air through the side teeth.
8. When you've had enough of this, stand up straight with your back to the door and, opening your eyes gently at first, slowly wake up in the place where you're sitting with this book.
9. Look around you constantly, up, down, in front of you, behind you, to your left and to your right. Observe the details. Has anything changed in the surrounding area?
10. Look natural and walk about the room holding a handkerchief.
11. Once you're upside down, do the splits with your legs and make a kicking motion with them. You should be pushing your legs round and then your whole bottom half will follow.
12. Then start to shake one of your hands rapidly – go on shaking it so rapidly that it builds up into an object which, not quite as solid-looking as that hand, is several times larger… weird isn't it?
13. Now think of a specific incident from your childhood.
14. Now think of another one.
15. And another one.
16. And another one.
17. And when you get up enough speed just let go…

The Lambent Itch of Innuendo

after W.B. Yeats

I will arouse angora nutmeg, and goitrous innuendo,
And a smirk cadenza bulwark, of cleak and weasel–coot ma'am;
Nitty bedposts will I hawfinch, ahoy for the homeopath,
And lob aloof in the beef–lucent glebe.

And I shanghai somewhere thereabouts, for peaky droning slipshod,
Droning from the vellum mosaic to whipjack the crockery;
There, mildew's allegorical and not a putrid goatskin,
And evolution fumbles the listless wistiti.

I will arouse angora nutmeg for aluminium nipplewort.
I heave lambent wax larrikins with lubricants by the shovelful.
While our Stan's on the rockery, or on the pawky groop,
I heave up on the departure lounge floor.

Whip Tim Kelly

for the Magnolia Warbler, Hairy Woodpecker and Tomm Lorenzin

Bipple-be-witsy-diddle
One, two, three, four, six
Qu'est ce qu'il dit?
Ra-vi-ol-i
Qu'est ce qu'il dit?
Po-ta-to chip

Quick, three beers
More pork, more pork
A little bit of bread and no cheese
No hope
highly variable – even whinny – in couplets

If I sees you, I will seize you and I'll squeeze you till you squirt
clear, liquid
Toot sweet
Drop-it, drop-it, cover-it-up, cover-it-up, pull-it-up, pull-it-up
and dip in flight
long drawn out stuttering
like a ping pong ball dropped onto a table
Poor Sam Peabody, Peabody, Peabody
O san pibbity, pibbity, pibbity

Who's awake? Me too
Quick, give me a rain check
Chuck Will's widow
Poor Will, Poor Will
Spit and see if I care, spit
Chi-ca-go, Chi-ca-go
Carolina, tea kettle, tea kettle
Carolina, tea kettle, tea kettle

Madge, Madge, pick beetles off, the water's hot
Who cooks for you?
Who cooks for you all?
Hip hip hurrah boys
Spring is here
Turdle-turdle-two-to-you
like a bathtub squeaky toy
but thinner

Last Gasp, At the

Who fixed Wragley's ricks?
Piffler Cabe, That
Man on the Island, That
Mr Quinn's Patagonian Lizard
Shut up in an Oven
Trapped by an Iceberg
Pursued by Malay Pirates
'Twixt Horns and Talons,
Pencil cases, 'Chums Day' and our 50,000
Horses of the Army, Jumping
Mr Minson, The mysterious
Salaries, Animals Earning Big
War balloons, At work with
Darkness, From out of the
Poses needing muscle and nerve
Cocoa-Nuts grow, Where the
Locomotives in out-of-the-way shapes
Fashioned by a Jack Knife
Come for a stroll down stream
Down stream, Come for a stroll
Stroll down stream, Come for a
Run-away Log Jam, On the
Precipice and the Parachute, The
Secret the Sea hid, The
Interrupted Plot, An

The Waterfall Illusion

There was something (a smell?) in the hedgerow.
I don't know what but it was alive
and giving itself in the dark.
That and the confusion of folksong
head and shoulders above all the earlier influences
like slag heaps
and they surely will.
The virus is spreading like an inkstain
under foot and up the spine
the 'h' silent and inarticulate
as clouds in the weft and waft
of a fine caravan site in Annan
where we simply hurled our excrement over the hedge
to the Falls of Foyers where in 1834 Dr Addams discovered that if
he stared for twenty seconds at a fixed point in the torrent, then
transferred his gaze leftwards to the adjacent rocky gully, the gully
appeared to shoot skywards.

This is all going on in my trousers remember
while St Jerome eats cheese and continues to read assiduously
in his study in the house on the lake, although the lake is
merely suggested by an expanse of unrippled brass
and the island itself is no bigger than the house that sits upon it.

It's market day and now we know this, everything changes.
An equestrian enters from the left, his horse playing the violin
extremely badly – even for a horse.
It is a music for all occasions, however, even this one.
Our necks twist effortlessly as my father is born again
in the living room this year, as in every previous year,
with all our legs across the table like it was midday
and there were no real people at all
only saints or tourists.

Who else would do this for you
in the middle of the Adagio
with your elbows for maximum effect?

Perhaps I should have said something else.
In one of the earlier drafts there was
a brass tap for one of the nipples,
a toad in the plughole.
The way her nose scrunches up
royalty on the patio.
The official prunes.

Just lying in bed and thinking about it.
This is the best part.
I should like to preface my remarks by declaring a lifelong interest
in the meat and livestock industry.

The Negatives

O you mountains cool and blue
Georg Trakl

O my valleys warm and red it is a greenhouse which is moving
                                        amongst the crowd.
It is a gargling stillness which puts brimming palaces within a
                                        rectangle.
How joyful this morning.

Within the city sobbing comes with tarnished broadsheets.
Bassoons are hooting, viridian green trousers are distinct.
In silvery dullness the knuckles expand and boil.

Gymnasts who probably thrive in the daytime
Write down simple memories of fish swimming.
Friends listen to one another firmly in the street.

A circle becomes cheerful, splendid and ornate;
Raised voices subside in hollows in the light.
Under the sea, cellar steps, anchors and a shawl are continuous.

Tree/Bush

TREE / BUSH

It can happen that three or four cross over each other so that one
has a knot in one's hand. Then there is a wound there then they
grow together.

STAIRS / LADDER

It is much more comfortable on the stairs than on the ladder.

STOVE / OVEN

The stove is what one has in the room.

LAKE / RIVER

Well the lake it can never be as long and never have that many
branches not in the least little bit.

GLASS / WOOD

Glass is a moss. You would have to make a hole in it unless it's a
dry twig. With glass you need to hit only twice.

FLY / BUTTERFLY

The fly has wings like glass.

(From Hans Asperger's paper on autism in childhood)

Blue

Raoul scrap iron begins with a 'mouth' and a 'moon'
from the same day is tulip red a poem, glass cheeks
yield lip and voice in my dwelling on the island's glad courage
whistling in the endless tuft and sparkling impossibility
throws in laconically a small brother of his own

American Experimental Music

Everything you can think of
all of the time
spread out in the hall

And at the other extreme
I am delighted to see
William and Mary

in and out of the piano
for hours at a time
during the breeding season

or pacing gingerly over the mud
in a piece called
Pacing Gingerly Over the Mud

Tring

from Gilbert White's Natural History of Selborne

My little intelligence is confined to the narrow sphere
of my own observations at home.

Swans turn white the second year, and breed the third.
Worms work most in spring.
Weasels prey on moles.
There are two sorts of eels in the Island of Ely.

Castration has a strange effect.
Parrots walk awkwardly.
Woodlarks hang poised in the air.
Starlings, as it were, swim along.

But the people of Tring, Hertfordshire
move in a buoyant manner,
as if lighter than air.
They seem to want ballast.

The enlargement of the boundaries

It has been my misfortune never to have had any neighbours
whose studies have led them towards the pursuit of natural
knowledge.

I have no acquaintance at present among the gentlemen of the Navy.
I have no friend left now at Sunbury.

What you mention with regard to reclaimed toads
raises my curiosity.

Not but now and then

I might perhaps dip and wash a little
and collecting all in skimming close
the land begins to think in woods tempered with salt
as summer declines all day long in the wet borders.

How strange is it in my field though
meeting a shoe, the face of the sky
darkening, drowned at an angle
and never seen till seldom squeals
the lakes and mill ponds building a rather rather
marooned in the steeples?

It is up to you Mr Crabtree.
I'd rather not raise their wings
and make them loquacious
late as Michaelmas, I am etc.
most shy and wild fine grasses.

The exhibition of the fishes

Quick dactyls, we observed, succeeded best
with a large speaking-trumpet held close to their hives
as fishes have no eyelids.

But we were still at a loss for
what is a sponge?
To most people it is a complete mystery.
There is still much we don't understand about sponges.
All the same a sponge is an animal.
The Breadcrumb Sponge is believed to be an annual.
A sweet polyglot.
Torquay.
Bournville.
Beginning of April.
St Hilda's Lodge.
Letchworth Women's Club.
In soft sunny weather
rising suspended and falling into
a large hollow space within a tall quick-set hedge
with the fishes swimming in a circle round it
and there is no doubt
the eggs are short and round this morning.

Mingles with the forest

And here I think will be the proper place to mention that
a pair of white owls, infested by little hanging ears, affright the ladies.

Lumping weight. We are twenty miles from the sea and almost as
                                                        many
from spring without the assistance of lime and turnips.

Turf the whisper, warble their throats aloof
as you propose, for the good of mankind, to be an active nimble fish
shivering a little with its wings when it sings so like a reed
and I make no ousels, no ousels from the North of England,
but belong to the side of a steep hill where we drink tea at one
with the churn chafers, shifting as well as flimsy, and therefore
the noise was from Edward's drawing.

I shall be glad about the mantelpieces
and on the bacon racks.

The plan was plausible
but I no longer wonder at the use of its middle toe.

I only know that

in the lane above Well-head, in the way to Emshot, they abound in the bank, in a darkish sort of marl; and are usually very small and soft; but in Clay's pond, a little farther on, at the end of the pit, where the soil is dug out for manure, I have occasionally observed them of large dimensions, perhaps 14 or 16 inches in diameter.

Before our beechen woods were so much destroyed we had myriads of them, reaching strings for a mile together as they went out in a morning to feed. When I was a little boy I recollect one coming now and then to my father's table. It ran I observed, with more dispatch than I was aware of, but in a most ridiculous and grotesque manner. I found it nailed up at the end of a barn, which is the countryman's museum. It was perfectly round, and about the size of a Seville orange, such are, I think, usually flat.

Before winter they harden and are able to shift for themselves. They are seen to come in flocks just before it is dark, and to settle and nestle among the heath on our forest. Another intelligent person assures me that they breed in great abundance all over the Peak of Derby.

This well accounts for the vast quantities that are caught on the South Downs near Lewes where they are esteemed a delicacy. Their livers, kidneys and hearts are large, and their bowels covered with fat. There are varieties of them, differing in colour; and some have fins up their tail and back, and some have not.

Their nostrils are bilobated, their shoulders broad and muscular, and their whole bodies fleshy and plump. Like Virgil's bees they drink flying. They also pick holes in apples left on the ground, and are much entertained with the seeds on the head of a sunflower. What they may do in the night I cannot say.

Cursu undoso

Gentlemen who have outlets might contrive to make ornament
subservient to utility and become so merry and loud as to be irksome
in a room where little is said but much is meant and understood.

Unlike the little girl who, as she was going to bed, always used to
                                      remark
'This district is an Anathoth, a place of responses or
echoes during the uncomfortable months of winter.'

From which I should suppose that the old ones do not always move
cursu undoso rising and falling in lovely curves around Lewes. And
                                      sounds
do not always give us pleasure according to their sweetness and
                                      melody.

But I think they do; and if they do, would they wash also?
I do not know anybody near the seaside that will take the trouble.
I shall say nothing further about it at present but it was

of a very clammy quality, so slimy and tenacious that eating
the scummings of pots and dashing into people's faces could by no
                                      means
be the approach of an absent lover foretelling rain before

retiring backward nimbly into their ovens and kneading troughs.
At length, a new relation (mother?) demands a new language
with a warning voice broad at the base and clanking

full of hollow vales and hanging woods.
Alcmæon does not advance what is true,
when he avers that goats breathe through their ears.

My female moose corresponds

Hedgehogs abound in my gardens and fields
and hurry our apples, pears, onions, potatoes, etc.
into the cellar and warm closets,
and the reason is plain, and perhaps
the later the hour the more so
with a bullet in a turnip field by moonshine.

'The Chinese word for dog to an European ear
sounds like "grig", "ling", "heath" and "furze", "goss" or "fern" and,
had the lake an arm or two more, "vast gluts of rain",'
says Eckmarck the Swede
with such a redundancy of upper lip as I never saw.

Monsieur Herrisant, a French anatomist, seems persuaded.
But the ingenious Mr Lisle carries it much further.
This basket will be in Fleet Street by eight this evening.

Please to let me hear if my female moose corresponds
with that you saw; and whether you think still
that the American Moose and European Elk are the same creature I am,

with the greatest esteem, etc.

of roads.

I long to see it.
great Gibraltar, swift in Tirol, without knowing it.
the belly and chin by ropes.
and snow.

ceilings.
lately.
prop the train, which is long and heavy when set on end.
somewhat into its mouth.

inquiry.
mice, refusing the red.
passage.
raw with oil and pepper.
in pursuit of the females.
after an ineffectual search in Linneaus, Brisson, etc.
gave it a ragged appearance.
feet above the butt.
in reality a bivalve.

I am able to say.
analogy.
of roads.
grass and leaves.
and the larger bats.

any advances.
one indeed and found it full of spawn.
a furlong or more.
tables nearly digested.
and laid up a good fund of materials for a future edition.

the mere accident of finding the potatoes.
or even the blue rag.
enough is a circumstance still more strange and wonderful.
safe and brisk in a glass decanter.
cut for watering the meadows.
in silence.
on such a restless tribe.

Hard references

Unlike copper

December soils
are hard references

Hence

just as Thomas Brown coppiced the wren
we should pocket all conspicuous wagtails

near Saffron
where the attempted reach drains the ear

Your Awful Voice

after Henry Purcell

Let the dreadful engines
Prattle, swell and rough seas employ
For this, there Etna, there
Come down, come away
Sound the trumpet, scold and scratch
Starve all within, reap with ease
On the sprightly hautboy play
In the groves, those flow'ry groves
Blue lightning

Down you must go
Luff, haul aft the sheet
Labour i'the quarries of a stony heart
Port, port, port for better or for worse
And bite beyond the tarpaulin boys

The mournful monarch she jilts all jollity
So unfit your revels
Her ends come away
And vex and scorn in hollow rocks
The wat'ry warble half so sweet

The skies with hands lift up his blessings
And bottle them out at sea

Pastoral

The folds shall be full of sheep, the valleys also shall stand so thick with corn
that they shall laugh and sing.

Psalm 65, v.13

A woman stands at a door
The thatch encrusted with moss
A valley winds deep down towards the sea
A figure reads by candlelight by a latticed window

And the moon
A full moon is shining
A huge golden moon
With an owl flying across its face

The moon has risen behind some lofty timber
The moon is scarcely clear of the hill
A tree springs up toward the moon
Dark clotted trees below the moon

And slightly above the moon
To the right of the moon
The moonlit slopes of the hill
A landscape with sheep

★

Sheep slightly drawn in pencil
A church with a boat and sheep
A flock of sheep in the foreground
With the hill sloping down from left to right
A cornfield sloping up from left to right
A woman reclining across the page from left to right
With her left hand on a Bible
And on the right a cartwheel

To the left the chimney and rooftop
Right, stooks of corn

Left, a cottage from which rises a wisp of smoke
Right, a stile
Left, a rabbit, a pool of water and a log
Right, a wall of trees crude & lumpy
Beyond right, a windmill

Otherwise snares
At right angles
In the twilight
Late twilight
Yellow twilight
Orange twilight is misleading
With yellow, green and pale blue
Interspersed with mauve shadows
And behind the green drapery
Walks a woman stepping on delicate herbage
A woman in a flowing red dress
Walks along a wall of gold and orange corn

And the woman's dress is blue
Seen through a tree
With a touch or two of pink
And some green mould

A woman in blue and red
One in red another in blue
One in white with a stick
One in green with a basket
And a man on the waggon
A parson in a cassock
And a ring of hurdles
Six sheep and two people

Two shadowy figures
Two men busy with sickles
Two oxen moving down a hill
Two wooden fences
Two delicate tree trunks, a stile, and a house
One cauldron with two brass lids and an Indian bell with whistles

More woods and hills
Three more versions of the same moon-and-hill theme above
Four holes in the hill
Three children
One epithet
Two on one sheet

On the ground a bearded man lies reading from a book loaded
With apples, bright red, touched, some of them, with white and
                                                          yellow light
And he largely experimented in egg vehicles & renders the whole
                                            system an alembic
of excrement and withal they can only pass slimy motions which
                                    do them no good

Three or four morsels of very fine ivory
Ten pages come from an oblong
Four people laughing
Three cattle in the lodge

while the hardened and still increasing faeces, which ought to be
got rid of, are as tense as a bronze cast in the mould of their peri-
staltics.

And some

have grape nuts
thrust upon them.

Poem beginning with a suggestion by Bengt Af Klintberg

When you walk into a forest don't forget to knock
so that you allow your surroundings to grow into you
and over your old home.

Five petals white. Yellow heart. Three leaves. Barren Strawberry.
Today I am feeling a little more accepted by the birds and rocks;
this damp cave in the moss.

Black plastic in the hawthorn branches is torn like a crow.
A blackcap sings whilst rearranging some of its feathers, not wholly
concentrating on its song as it pushes up through cracks in the
                                                        pavement.

'To wander' is the Taoist codeword for becoming ecstatic
purple vetchling, curlew rising from the field through fulsome
lute playing in the sheepfold then settling back down again

into my Samuel Palmer Magic Apple Tree armchair
in The Shed: for people who work in sheds
or shed-like atmospheres.

Being big

I spent most of my time in the cowshed listening
while the Wooster girls would sit on the walls
wearing little white caps and coats.

Will opened the window and out they flew
and the smells began to come off the fields of mangle.

Things looked more real in the school.
There were round tables, I think two,
an ordinary stove, a sort of egg,

the old lady and the mysterious effect
she had on me, making paper nuns,

rooks flying home
getting under the table
and under the bed,

where the cracks in the floor
were rather like an orchard
with cardboard ladders leaning against the trees
and little figures going up into them.

And out of it would rise my elder sister
by the mantelpiece practising her viola,
making a most lovely shape.

I remember the shape well –
a sort of great triangular shape.

And behind that, you would usually
see an attic or kitchen, or when a garden,
it was the back garden with the walnut tree
changing one room into another.

The Call of the Drum and the Slap of Glory

after Rumi

Come to the orchard in spring.
Sit here beside me. I have a secret to tell you.
Be clear now and quieter than a dove.

I saw you last night at the gathering.
It was midnight.
The whole neighbourhood up and out
peering into the faces of travellers.

Every image is a lie – dissolving.
A hand shifts our birdcages around
and the little hanging lamps.
I think I'm in love
I lose my place
                        the shape of my tongue

    Shhh…

Set fire to your friends
and his friend the goldsmith
can prune the weary boughs.

I am God, a thirsty man
running into the sea and the sea
cries easily like a little child waiting
for dawn and the noise of the door opening.

And now silence my strict tutor
is another man sleeping in the cemetery.
The dark thought, the shame, the malice.

His body lies empty. Tents billow on the beach.
The caliph drops his cup, closes your mouth.
The day is cold, absent-minded but sober.
The world is too full to talk about
and never leave the premises.

This is far enough, a glass of wine, the door
and the doorkeeper will go unused.
A thread flows from minaret to bird to your hair
as a man walks into an orchard in spring.

Kabir says

after Kabir's Ulatbamsi — 'Upside-down songs'

The world is a fishnet
And who will believe it?

As it is
So it is
This way and that

Give him a drink
For only a great big fish
Could swallow everything

A dreamer wakes from sleep
The dog hides under the haystack
You're blowing through bamboo
No one looks in at your door

Lust and delusion
Water the roots
Only this, only this, only this
In four directions

The banks are swimming loose talk
The thread gets wet, the warp is wrecked

There is no hope for the bridesmaid
Is a lizard that yields butter
But peddles camphor and runs
From both when she can

The fruit is sweet but so far
So are all the others

Can a tailor mend it?
I have my doubts

A Man in the Wings

I am tired of saying a man in the wings
as a frantic dog in a glass temple
rules piety like a parrot on a pole

A stream of ice-cold dimensions
demands no room
for people darken

Futt! The high-class lady is filled with wheels

A deep red
life-size rector checking the yawns
let us say
with a white handle

You never know when or where
when out they come holding the rope

Who's to blame?

Three villages
I eat
to fill the land

The sea rolls
The mind goes hunting
from house to house
building the distillery
as your yellow face shrivels

I ask you

The bee has flown
tired of pleasing the eyes

The frog is sleeping
utterly shrewd

The Yellow Orioles are equals now

after Wang Wei

And you, my loose palace moat
Must relax last season's crop at dusk

How lovely those drifts
Making you wait calmly behind

The rain red and yet green
Where the spring wind obliged

Birthday Haibun

i.m. Roger Deakin

The river's quieter now. So I can hear it. Before, further upstream where the river rushed over and around boulders and down falls, the sound seemed to fill my head completely – the whole landscape too. Now, because I can hear other things, like the thin calls of some goldcrests and the occasional piping of a wagtail, I can also hear the river.

> to the wagtail
> the river sounds like
> the front door swinging open

A dipper would fit that better but I haven't seen one yet. I know they must be out there somewhere – it's perfect territory – but I'd somehow feel dishonest using one without having seen it first. I'm told there are otters along this river too.

> to the otter
> the river sounds like
> an Ordnance Survey map unfolding

Of course, I haven't seen an otter either – ever in fact – but I'm starting to relax. I've just been swimming. It was painfully cold and, even when my breathing returned to normal after a couple of minutes in the water, much of my body, especially my ankles, still ached with the cold. But sitting on the bank of the river now the air is beautifully warm and I'm enjoying the flood of endorphins coupled with the secret pleasure of not wearing any pants under my jeans. I'm forty-four today and I don't have to write a poem. I don't have to do anything.

> to the river
> the flood of endorphins
> sounds familiar

The river is slow and clear and brown as the tea in a teapot. Little islands of froth float by on the surface of the water and water-boatmen manoeuvre jerkily between them. On the far bank there's a yellow wagtail fidgeting. I wonder why they wag their tails and then notice that it isn't. It's *tapping* it up and down. I've known smokers tap their cigarettes like that, constantly, so that the ash doesn't get the chance to accumulate.

Several Senryu

1
no longer a caterpillar
the great blue heron
is preparing our tea

2
in a darkened room
the barnacled rocks
have all gone berserk

3
wherever I look
the indifference
of Mexican hats

4
one must kneel to see
the tiny goldfish
is no longer there

5
the lofty eagle
a dry formality
in a polka dot waistcoat

6
a moment ago
scooting madly round the floor
without any necks

7
I've grown tired of being
the smell of the sea
and then just ignored

8
the monastery bell
it echoes across the creek
and then back again

9
all of a sudden
in the kitchen
combing the dog

10
heralded by birds
composed of gravel
used as a sofa

11
emerging from fog
the hummingbird veers
into my teeth

12
right now, this is it
gather in one tree
and share eggs

The North Cumbrian Coast

from H.E. Winter's Cumbrian Coast: A History

We begin our tour at ROCKCLIFFE on the Solway marshes. Here on 25 January 1796, several houses were swept away by an exceptional high tide. In November 1938 about 1,000 sheep were drowned on the marshes when there was a 24ft tide and gale.

It was at nearby CARGO that King Edward I died on 7 July 1307. In 1685 an inscribed pillar was set up on the site of the king's death but it fell down in 1795.

We next visit BURGH-BY-SANDS. There are old gravestones in the churchyard and an old yew tree.

A little further west in DRUMBURGH, the one-time Methodist Chapel is now a house.

Next is PORT CARLISLE. A canal to here from Carlisle was opened on 12 March 1823 and drained in 1853. It cost about £90,000 to construct and was never a financial success.

At the point of land where Hadrian's Wall began stands BOWNESS-ON-SOLWAY. The Solway Viaduct was built here in 1869. It was damaged by ice in the winter of 1875 and closed in 1921 due to its unsafe condition.

We next come to ANTHORN. The name means 'thorn bush' and in the village close to a stream is an old thorn bush.

To the west of Anthorn is CARDURNOCK where there are just a few houses and farms.

Near the outfall of the river Wampool into Moricambe Bay is KIRK-BRIDE. There is a village hall.

A little to the south is NEWTON ARLOSH.

A little further to the south is ABBEYTOWN, site of the greatest abbey in Cumberland. On 1 Jan. 1600 at 3p.m. the tower collapsed and much of the church was destroyed. On 18 April 1604 the roof caught fire and it was burned out and became a ruin.

NEW MAWBRAY was pillaged by the Scots in 1216 and 1322.

Proceeding north we come to SKINBURNESS. In 1301 the whole village was swept away in a violent storm.

South of Skinburness is SILLOTH-ON-SOLWAY. Silloth used to have a wooden lighthouse called 'Tommy Legs'. In the late 1870s the North British Railways was unable to maintain the town's sewers. This had a detrimental effect on Silloth's popularity and it fell into a decline.

Further south is BECKFOOT where a Friends' meeting house was closed in 1940.

Finally, we come to ALLONBY, a popular seaside resort with an ancient and varied history. At the leisure centre during July and August there is an Egg Dump and Karaoke with the resident DJ every Friday night.

Noses and Feet

Can I make a painting about the human spirit without
having to paint noses and feet?

Albert Irvin

What might be the lower half of a woman's face
or a boat or some clouds is all deliberately suggested
but never defined, as a little boy,
totally engrossed in his game of cards, dissolves
into currents of line and patterns of coiling
tendrils, aquatic plants, spores, fungi and a snafu
of tangled film negatives that is forever
beginning at the beginning as we move through them
towards a quiet place where it is possible to breathe
and smell the salt upon the air, feel the wind
cold on our cheeks and remember something
which, to avoid getting all cluttered up,
we had forgotten once in a Persian miniature.

And so we come to the length of hose which
we'll use later on to make a garden of rainbows,
with a system of sprinklers and lights to shine through them.
In the middle of the night the house will be surrounded
by fans of water, light and colour.
It won't *be* a house, of course, but we'll read it as one.

Leaving me

in the dark
in the museum
on the twelfth floor
in an old egg carton
all folded up
with no money
in my navel
in the lightning flash
of the mirror
where my sister slept
on the Chinese ginger jar
on a white plate
on the kitchen table
deep within the stream
within the lily
in the temple
straining at the padlock
before my eyes
on the mantelpiece
on the lake's shore
overwhelmed by mist
between her breasts
moulded with snow
scattered with clams
after miles and miles
drifting out of the mist
across the stillness of the pool
through an open window
in the broken curve
of the empty cup
at the end of myself

Poetry should be made by all (ii)

after Benjamin Péret

Take in your hand, ink, and a pen with a new nib and settle
comfortably at your table. Forget all your preoccupations, forget
that you are married, that your child has whooping cough, forget
that you are a Catholic, forget about literature from any place in
the world and period in history,
forget your father and your mother
forget imperial mints
forget your name
forget what you are about to do
forget enigmatic smiles
forget the vast room whose floor was covered in furs
forget my extreme arousal
forget snowflakes
and champagne
forget your right hand
forget the poor fishermen who didn't catch a single fish
forget the field of buttercups where you found your children
forget the horizon
forget lungs
forget the bogs and chasms
forget 1936
forget lying in the hammock
forget her eyes
forget her footprints on the beach
forget stilts
forget that goats are a source of adhesiveness
forget here and there
forget the smallest pebble
forget its special quality with a snort
forget the cormorant's eye
sea urchins
white heat
forget that as it dissolves it increases in size
forget the earth every evening
forget its natural cavities

forget the customers
forget the pinetrees under the snow
forget pretty holes in the clothing
so green and so white
forget Bavaria
forget rolling me along naked like a barrel, my arms pinned against
my buttocks
please try
forget to my dismay the ground floor
forget up and down
forget hinges
forget the chestnut vendor
forget 'Just let me fix my hair and I'll be right with you.'
forget 'Took off to whom?'
forget to curl up
forget dripping from the gutters
forget the hole through which the man had entered
forget his cries of rage
and how wonderful it was later
...in the water
forget surrealism
forget tree frogs
forget strange methods of getting into and out of
forget Vivian's bargain
forget Zanzibar, stirring times in
forget fancy mice
perch fishing
Edgbaston
the *Lusitania*
forget how I won the Commodore's cup
or how I came to be a doctor in the forest – the land and people of
Ogowe
forget yours sincerely
no really, forget it.

This said let me begin:

Pendolino

I am sitting on a train and there is a low evening sun shining through the window on my left. There is also rain – a heavy April shower – so the window is covered with raindrops that are running diagonally down the glass because of the speed of the train.

I am looking at the back of the seat in front of me. I don't know what it is made of – some sort of grey slightly reflective material – a kind of metal or hard plastic perhaps. The sun is shining through the window and onto the back of the seat so that the raindrops on the window are projected onto it – the shadows of the drops that is.

I have read about the semi-abstract films of Stan Brakhage but have never seen one and so I decide to watch one now. I imagine I am sitting in a tiny cinema with just one seat and a screen above my knees. And I settle down to this private viewing of the rain.

But after a while I start to wonder about the films of Stan Brakhage. I wonder how long they might last and whether there would be a soundtrack and then I notice that these raindrops are really fat and when their shadows streak across the back of the chair they seem to have tails stretched out behind them. Like sperm – sperm in a hurry for something. An egg, I suppose, would be normal. Only they don't look like they are searching for an egg to me. They just look like they want to escape – to flee the scene. There is almost a sense of panic.

And then the back of the seat comes into focus again. It has the colour and shape of a gravestone and the shadows of the raindrops start to look like words being scribbled frantically across the grave-stone by some unseen hand.

And then I start to think this is really coming together; a gravestone; the shadow of the rain writing on it, 'one whose name was writ in water' etc. But then I notice the gravestone has a handhold on the aisle side, shaped a bit like a Mickey Mouse ear.

A gravestone with a cartoon ear is no good to me so I look out of the other window and see a small copse on the far side of the valley. I recognise it. It is the clump of oak trees that welcomes me home every time I travel this way. It is the shape of a rough triangle and each time I see it I think of pudenda, 'the hidden parts'; 'that of which one ought to be ashamed'.

And the truth is I do feel a little ashamed. But of what? Of imagining a woman's genitals in a landscape owned by the National Trust? Of imagining the wrong woman's genitals perhaps? Of not being sure when it is correct to refer to pudenda and when to pudendum no matter how many times I look it up in the dictionary? Of not being on a train at all now but here at my desk, repeatedly looking up pudenda and pudendum in the dictionary while pretending to be sitting on a train and seeing things?

Or is it simply that I am ashamed of the fact that it is only when I leave home and then come back to it that I want to write these days? Am I Rumi's foolish man 'In Baghdad dreaming of Cairo; in Cairo dreaming of Baghdad' searching for treasure in distant cities only to return at last and find it buried under my own house?

Not really. What is there to be ashamed of, after all, in trying to follow Reverdy's directions by learning 'to love reality better after a long detour by way of dreams'? I ask you? I ask you in particular, R.H. Stacy, Associate Professor of Russian Literature at Syracuse University, poised there on the back flap, perusing your own half-read book and thoughtfully smoking an unlit pipe. You look like you might know a thing or two about this.